Blu Baaalloo

10 years of me

By Lisa Ieraci

Order this book online at www.trafford.com
or email orders@trafford.com

Most Trafford titles are also available at major online book retailers.

Note for Librarians: A cataloguing record for this book is available from Library
and Archives Canada at www.collectionscanada.ca/amicus/index-e.html

Printed in Victoria, BC, Canada.

ISBN: 978-1-4269-1846-9 (sc)

ISBN: 978-1-4269-1847-6 (dj)

Library of Congress Control Number: 2009937383

*Our mission is to efficiently provide the world's finest, most comprehensive book publishing
service, enabling every author to experience success. To find out how to publish your book, your
way, and have it available worldwide, visit us online at www.trafford.com*

Trafford rev. 9/9/2009

 www.trafford.com

North America & international
toll-free: 1 888 232 4444 (USA & Canada)
phone: 250 383 6864 ♦ fax: 812 355 4082

Dedication

* To my authentic self *
&
* the one who cannot fail
*

" *peace not pieces* "

I

Send You

Love And Light

From The Earth Plane,

I Shine Through The Darkness

& Open Your Eyes

So You May See The Truth.

I Bring To Light That You Are Free.

You Are Safe Now!

So Be It!

It Is

*

PREFACE

I was once what you would call a quite complex person…
Throughout my journey
I believed firmly in six words.

Together they convey the one lesson by which I lead my journey
&
the base foundation on which I wrote this book.

"THE TRUTH WILL SET YOU FREE"

Each verse translates a segment of my history,
or in this case as it were…
"my-story".

So welcome to the inside story,
behind the scenes of my so called mind…
into the depths of a place even I many times have second guessed
treading…

Welcome to my heart.
Welcome to my thoughts.
Welcome to my
Blu Baaalloo.

ACKNOWLEDGEMENTS

Much love and appreciation to my family,
thank you for your support and patience!

To the many helpers along my journey.
Without you all I would have never experienced, loved,
raged and in turn been inspired.
You know who you are...
Thank you! I will love you all ways!

Many thanks to Giovanna Zappia my editor,
your push was definitely in the right direction.

And thank you…

The reader!
For bringing my dream
closer to completion.

Peace be with you...

May your truth set you free!

Contents

CHAPTER ONE

Purr-Spective

Present

Although it seemed that he had lost,
A thaw did come due to the frost.

A recipe preserved in time,
A manifesting gift of rhyme.

And joint were forces to retrieve,
All thoughts of lack were but perceived,
A bounty brought by whom believed,
Stocks replenished though you had grieved.

I bring from nothing just for you,
What you thought lacking I renew.

So have a faith that fails not.
In dreams a mind can change the plot.

Simply ask that's what to do,
So think and see it come to you.

It isn't hopeless you will find,
All you need do is…

CHANGE YOUR MIND!!*

Dec 2008

Angelic

Nowhere to run, nowhere to hide,
with consciousness comes a chance to decide.

Near in control trying to change,
the real world once so far,
now just within range.

The journey fades...
to be untold,
upon reaching,
time & space.

How could all truth now forbidden be?

or divine ever be...
dis-placed?

09/02/1998
20/04/2009

I

Sitting here I reminisce,
recalling years long past.
Questioning the actions,
that I prayed would never last…
in minds of friends, as well as foes,
secrets of shame,
they could expose!

A future placed in jeopardy,
unfortunate this be!
Especially when the guilty party
begins and ends with me!

Decisions, which were blindly led,
By others trained to burn…
Whatever little innocence,
Remained with no concern!

17/02.2000

Re-Cycling

A smile shinning brightly,
but still no one can see...
the goddess trapped beneath the walls,
somewhat resembles me.

A soul of blind perfection's,
exposed by common law.
An individual miracle,
disguised by bad re pour.

Conflict braised with circumstance,
intentions led astray.
Aggravating solitude,
which keeps the soul at bay.

With multitudes of questions,
and answers true and wise.
Amazement was restored to thee,
as was learnt compromise.

The clock at which we set ourselves,
still ticks it's own tick-tock.
The secrets lie within ourselves,
to which we must unlock.

Perspectives that we can escape,
are devious and sly.
It's not ourselves that we should look,
but, at the passers by.

For life is but a slide show,
of which we choose the scene.
It's not that boy, who's being rude,
it's us that's being mean.

The way the public come to be,
is purely through our minds.
Our souls must learn to break away,
and cut these fleshy binds.

Our maker will one day rise up,
torch bright will lead the way.
Supply the tools explain the rules,
BEWARE or you will stray.

Embrace each and every lesson,
as if it were last breath.
For the torture you endure on earth,
is reviewed upon your death!!!!

25/11/2000

? Question Calling ?

What does this great world
hold for
me?

Each turn shedding
more mystery.

As I wander round
aimlessly.

With truth untold
and hard to see.

Unheard by all to which
I plea.

Can't seem to find
my destiny!

1/ 2001

Return Trip

Travelling cross these barren lands,
I watch as wind blows dessert sands,
the darkness blankets all I see,
it's depth thick with intensity.

As scenes fly by, my deep thoughts strain,
ego yes you've struck again,
my mind is blank no thoughts relay,
my passion thieved and kept at bay.

This battle you must instigate,
has kept me from my makers gate,
the arms of love I once had known,
I tried to leave and go alone.

Now my spirit must return,
and from this recent lesson learn,
though as my soul starts to remember,
my spirit ego must dismember.

Alone though surrounded,
my solitude crowded,
the blanket which I clutch to my chest,
my only protection from night as I rest.

Such cold dark nights are but a warning,
that just as light will break the morning,
dark cold death will one day end,
light leading us home safe again.

1/ 2001

Wake Up Time

Alone I call out in the darkness,
Embraced are we who know the truth.
Exiled to our cruel place of darkness,
accused are we that need no proof.

The dream you judge and execute,
is not the dream at all.
Though listening to majority,
you'll miss your makers call.

Realize in everything you see,
the meaning has been taught.
Your ego will hit self-destruct,
but spirit can't be bought.

Convinced are you, that we exist,
and all is well as well.
The mistake we have made alas,
is this my friend...is hell.

Now if you're sitting in your chair,
quite comfy and content.
I probably quote you when I say,
That "hell ain't bad get bent".

Unfortunately this won't do,
life's lessons seek to teach...
It's back at home where we belong,
right out of cruel hell's reach.

1/ 2001

Mecca-Maze

Robots lay dormant,
in sweet dreams of torment.

Programmed destruction,
unscathed by obstruction.

Entangled in life,
cut sharp doth the scythe.

But not sharp enough,
engulfed in the rough.

Will humanity remain,
as deer would lay lame.

Frightened and scared,
until all truths are bared.

01-02-2001

Caught Up In Time

Time spins a web,
of sunshine and deceit.

A solitary rat race,
which is run by the elite.

Enticed we're drawn,
like moth to flame.

And lost is he,
that plays times game.

01-02-2001

Soul Seduction

Kiss the breeze,
caress the clouds,
make love to the sun.
Fly through to oblivion on my smooth scarlet wings.
I offer complimentary passage to you,
jumping on,
together we flew.
Now wave good-bye,
farewell, so-long.
As the life you once embraced is gone!
You failed to ask or question dear,
blind faith you had in thee,
and now I'll explain to your highness,
the cost of this voyage so free,
as now is too late for a refund,
your sweet soul is my property.
Why do you weep sweet child?
You know all things come with a price.
So welcome I do you to my world,
I think I can spare you a slice.
If only you realized how precious,
and tasty and sweet is your soul.
If weren't for my coming along,
the world may have taken it's toll!
And then you may or may have not,
appreciated what it's like.
To have yourself subjected,
as it's placed upon my spike.
So let this be a lesson learned!
To every stomach which has churned.
With gifts accepted be concerned.
You play with coals you will get burned!!!

23/08/2001

"Some Thing For Kate"

Alone in the silence a shadow was
born,
it's mind untouched and pure.
With but one objective to pierce
through these times,
deceit such as this knows no cure.

The seed of deception,
was carelessly sown.
Carefully cultivated,
the sweet seed has grown.

Maybe she's true,
or maybe she's not.
But one thing's for sure...
She cant be forgot!

4/2001

?<?? At What Cost ??>?

Intentions which were led astray,
with lines so thin to cross.

A young girls hopes are washed away,
entwined she danced with loss.

Blinded was she by fairy gifts,
subsided was her fear.

Engulfed was she in life's harsh rifts,
then lost all she'd held dear.

Remorse was not an option,
She drank forbidden sweat.

The Devil's sweet concoction,
Of lust, pain and regret.

01-05-2001

Royal-Tease

Interpret the shades of aqua rays,
filter debris on silver trays,
the rush you will, but rarely stays,
when this compulsion steals your days.

Time takes a trip inside your room,
falling into this empty spoon,
breakthrough the sweat and taste the
fume,
fate sealed seduction by what you
consume.

Gliding on through untouched and
alone,
with the scars you've come to own,
seeking support you said you'd
outgrown,
her majesty crowned on addictions
throne.

13/09/2001

Separated
States

I found my separated state,
alone lost in the cold.
With heavy feet it dragged along,
it's face deep lined and old.

It disappeared in shadows,
created by the night.
To only be exposed by rays,
of silver lunar light.

Not fear of dark nor love to shine,
illuminated thee.
Though, as time excreted seconds fell,
incriminating she.

Who was this lady stepping on,
the boogie man's long toes?
What was the act so innocent,
from which suspicion rose?
Where were the words put into verse,
so flaws were there to find?
The answer's paranoia from,
your separated mind.

10/ 2001

Why Do You Dance?

Lift The Veil My Sweet Prince,
And Peer Deep Down Inside.

You Know That You Must Search For Truth,
Life's Laws Are Wrong They Lied.

In My Eyes Shine A Love So True,
It's Purest Of Pure.

But Still I Find You Dance My Love,
Behind The Veils Lure.

You Can Set Our Spirits Free,
& Be The One Who Saves...

The Innocent Unconscious Sons,
From The Temporal's Shallow Graves.

17/7/2001

Anything But EFO

Sweet cool breeze you know no
bounds,
move through the skies,
creating the sounds,
to which we retreat,
when the cities and towns,
destroy our minds peace,
when commotion surrounds.

The world you embrace and float
through so free,
ignore your sweet blessings,
although not the tree,
it swishes to your music,
so secretly.

Dancing it sways,
showing to we,
who count no importance,
of what we can't see.

12/09/2001

Dedication To Soar

Oh wise eagle,
spirit of the sky.

Teach to me your wisdom,
let me follow as you fly.

Fill my mind with knowledge,
my eyes with light and truth.

Bring me to the point,
where I no longer ask for proof.

I am prepared to journey,
with you and know no doubt.

I am prepared to soar with you,
and learn what life's about.

04/2001

Socialists

Why do the greatest blessings,
come from the harshest trials?
How can the sweetest poetry,
be born through tears not
smiles?

Ironic this life seems to be,
with all it's twists and turns.
Corrupting love destroying
dreams,
must be its chief concerns.

Revolving on its axis,
this great hypocrisy.
Enslaved by the consumer
world,
it's our society.

13/09/2001

South Surprise

As sands blow over time,
a voice you claim to be,
does echo from another time,
against the crashing sea.

A transformation flyer,
sweeps low across the grain.
What they would call reality,
I'd rather call insane.

I came to see you in a dream,
and you did think it real.
Previewing but a film clip,
you reached forth and broke the seal.

Much like what you'd expected,
excelling through great strain,
how many times was this to be?
And what was my next reign?

In this dual world it's hard to see,
especially with blind eyes.
And though still here I now am free,
I caught me by surprise.

I showed myself that I am one,
and will forever be...
with God until this dreams undone,
and all my selves are free!

21/10/2001

Dream Gift

A gift for you my daughter sweet,
a playpen for your fun!
Now don't forget its all a dream,
and dreams can be undone!

Although firm warnings were in place,
Lovely lost her head.
And mothers words so helpful,
from her memory quickly fled.

And so she delved in deeper,
making much a playful mess.
The shroud of cobwebs closed right in,
and thoughts of home were less.

New ideas and roles to play,
became loves chief concern.
With all the fun and games around,
for mother would she yearn?

Well, loves dream play rolled right along,
and in no time at all.
The make believe reality,
drowned out her mother's call.

The costumed scenes and sequin dreams,
illusion's hooks deep in!
Now so lost, loves trapped in sleep,
believing in fake skin.

Though meanwhile, in reality,
Love's mother watches on.
Peacefully she smiles,
for her child is not gone.

But in the dreamy state for Love,
it's not the case at all.
This shell shocked Cinderella,
is at Ego's beck and call.

Wake up you sleeping beauty!
for matter can't be found.
Perfected for your pleasure,
enticed and trapped you're bound!

What once had seemed so innocent,
a barter of the soul.
Was now a non-existing game,
of which love must control.

12/5/2002

Fell 4 It

"Well howdy there stranger,
you're looking kinda lost"

"Come sit down by,
the side that lie,
and wager,

what's your cost?"

Falling from grace,
I stepped up the pace.
I blindly jumped in and entered the race.

Losing my place,
lost gone not a trace.

Now hiding my face,
in dream-scapes of lace.

26/05/02

Dream On

If there's no such thing as future,
and the past has never been…
then this place we know as present,
is alas a waking dream.

So how did we come to enter,
this so called dreamy state?
What is this thing we're looking for?
Where is the exits gate?

And if we can't remember…
what exactly we have lost,
how do we recognise it,
when our path this it does cross?

Somewhere beneath the heavy sheets,
the truth and answers lay…
amongst Gods sleeping children,
lost in dreams another day.

12/09/04

Fate Hearted

Right on the verge,
of half way up,

With dream fulfilled,
and deluged cup.

Watching flow,
above the rim,

Intention high,
with odds so slim.

Alas it seemed to be too much,
To stand alone without a crutch.

Somewhere along the journey,
revisited again..

Came on the realisation
which stared...
not back an end.

Some how the great perspective,
flowed forth from idle state.

Within the single reckoning...
''twas I that sealed my fate.

2006

Barabis

Impossible a notion...
how truth when crucified,
despicable the concept,
true love...
then nullified?

Is all that I,
solely extend.
but of myself?
unto the end?

How can an offer bona fide,
from a real place then be denied?

Where's all that was,
turned in but to,
a slight of what it all but knew?

In altered states,
that's where the scores,
are tallied,
Turning wins to draws.

A place that is will never be,
but in the light of truth to see!

Something that was will never last,
as it exists in what has past.

An actual real live warranty,
is only certified if we...
Can hold our soul as life's receipt,
walking in truth, lessons complete.

04/10/06

Lone Star

Waiting,
for what seemed eons,

I burned and drifted far...
Across the space of consciousness,
A lone and wandering star.

The walls projected,
oh so far,
So far not even I,
Could reach forth to another,
across,
the once filled starlit sky.

Isolation chosen,
with blinkers on I sped.
Into the depths of loneliness,
Where solo fliers tread.

That which offers no resistance
Can often be harder to push,
Far from forbidden apple,
Long past the burning bush

So far into the void,
Creating, dreams unknown.
No audience to share with me,
For the splendour is my own.

1/4/07

So Called Friends

Truths are spoke In riddles,

lies are freely flown.

Contesting all creation,

The whistle never blown.

Intrinsic forms now walk,

In shoes the fallen own,

The usurpers ever waiting,

To steal the good Kings throne.

In shadows they do circle,

awaiting but the chance,

for their own taste of glory,

Ascending they advance.

Wide open the unknowing,

The stealth caught in a glance,

Tangible acts envisioned,

tis' the devil's own in trance.

9/4/07

Blind

In my head was all I knew,
of how and what I thought was true.

In my heart was all I'd see,
Though blind this friend I'd found in me.

In my mind illusions reigned,
A clouded judge in me I blamed

In my soul a truth did stare,
Through emerald eyes,
it was aware.

In my life head, heart and mind,
ruled me until I could not find,
the truth that lay deep in my eyes,
relentless they'd not compromise.

As crazed as it may've seemed at times,
Side stepping,
dodging hazard signs.

Upon the time it seamed so strange,
to know and not foresee a change.

My eyes were useless I did find…
as two of three to love turned blind.

CHAPTER TWO

Emo

Vegetable

Endless bouts,
of constant doubts.
Escalation.
Imitation.
Now retain as words do strain.

Insert the card,
when you discard,
the speech unspoke;
what did provoke?
The silent air, the harsh cold stare,
were you aware?
Was I?

Call we do
for love so true.
Through foreign tone the means have flown.

If only thee,
could see

or maybe,
just agree,

that silence is our plea...

FOR LOVE

04-05-2001

Sum Tare

Somewhere lost, with no direction.

An empty heart, with no reflection.

With no contempt, the lines were drawn.

A yearning heart, slowly was torn.

The deepest tear, silently shed.

The softest step, so light to tread.

So much to gain, too much to lose.

But still this option, we'd abuse.

A growing, burning, nurtured seed.

Who ever knew, two hearts would bleed.

2000

Dearest Angel

Angel of God reveal to me,
the secrets of the past and see...
The words unspoken, can't be defined,
the secrets told, untrue and blind.

Denied by a stranger, shunned at the door.
Tried and quickly executed,
by uneducated law.

Communication breakdown,
wounds now too deep to heal.
A reputation tarnished,
what once was love now steel.

Individual tendencies, narrow minded lies.
Attempts of contact intervened,
despite the numbered tries.

An absence inexcusable,
a bridge not built to cross,
imprisoned with cold solitude and self inflicted loss.

Abandoned when most weakest,
a thorn plucked from the side.
A coat of armour now in place,
for all feelings to hide.

Now two stars so far apart,
burn and drift away.
The hours days and years may pass,
but treasured memories stay!

23-10-2000

Love Junkie

Disappeared from sight you did,
behind dense walls,
to where you hid...
the words that speech could not pronounce,
of love once strong but now renounced.

Exposed when most curious,
two strangers leapt in.
Tasting the fruit, condoning the sin.
And then without thought,
a young girl was bought.
With just one reward,
to service her lord.

Lost then she was, in a game called his mind.
And seek did she exits,
though when reached declined.
She floated through life aimlessly,
as boat would minus oar.
Amazed by musty points of view,
and attitudes so poor.

Yet she could not,
seem to break the spell.
Had years gone by?
She could not tell.
She looked about her private hell
and then realized
how far she fell.

01-04-2001

Don't Be Nasty

Trying to accomplish a mission un-described,
by laws or common knowledge,
or feelings un-prescribed.
A new refreshed perspective coincidence exposed,
so many things to be discussed,
so much left un-proposed.
A limbless man attempting stride,
the blind leading the blind.
Enticed, coerced and dragged away,
tempted to change your mind.
A labyrinth with so many twists,
at what price would you pay?
For just a peek at what's inside
how much is it to play?
Believe me not, the price is meek,
it's nothing much at all.
If you play you only risk your demise and your fall.
I hope I haven't scared you!
Don't doubt this offers wealth!
Discretion is essential!
I'll keep it to my self!
The offers on the table,
please join me in my lair.
There is but one thing left to ask...
Are you willing to dare?

03-05-2001

Quiet Company

I can't understand why the silence hurts!
It's searing pain,
Its empty tears,
Its lonely cries.

I can't comprehend, why it's here with me!
Imploring my love,
shredding my mind,
bleeding my heart.

I can't seem to see through the keyhole,
to which only you hold the key.
You throw the switch to my electric chair,
wrapping my soul like a car round a tree.

And there in the silence I find...

the empty tears imploring my love,

the searing pain shredding my mind,

the lonely cries bleeding my heart.

Here in the silence I find,

your favourite gift to me,

LONELINESS.

03/08/2001

Sun-Fall

Her sun would not listen,
when she told him to beware.
Insanely he persisted,
and jumped right into their lair.

The stakes were high.
The thrill was meek.
But still this danger he did seek.

She fought to save,
though efforts grave,
she could not save,
her wiley knave.

So through cold nights,
she sat alone.
Unable to expose,
to he who she awaited,
as her bold efforts were tainted,
by his shrewd and vicious foes.

The star's bright light was darkened,
to the one which needed most.
Her room was cold and lonely,
as she now was silence' host.

And there she sat subjected,
to times game now infected.
Her love waiting to drown,
on the day the sun went down.

04/09/2001

Return Serve

To abandon the warmest touch,
to abuse a faith so blind.
To accuse an open heart,
to accept and then to bind.

You torture all I place before,
behind or by your side.
You sense it all in retrospect,
and I wholly abide.

Commute we do on rusty gages,
attraction distorts,
as you speed read the pages,
why try to appear while your side stepping
stages,
creating your world,
so we'll share separate cages.

Now that is how your race is run,
so point match set all to the sun,
and when your game is played and won,
you'll see my game has just begun!!!

08/09/2001

Think

I'm thinking about you.

Your emerald green eyes,
gleaming in the darkest room.

Your warm soft breath on my neck,
as you hold me close in your sleep.

Your soft lips murmuring "I love you",
when you stir from your dreams.

I'm thinking about you.

Your words so wise and insightful,
translating your thoughts with such brilliance.

Your infant like manner when you tire,
and need me to help you let go.

Your ridiculously cheerful grin,
when presented with a simple tray of pizza.

I'm thinking about you.

And all we had and were.
Holding on fast to a moment,
upon once a time now a blur.

I'm trying to not think about you.

As the void you once filled now does seep.
Your face is engraved in my memories,
and voice it does call in my sleep.

I can't seem to not think about you.

Why must letting go be so hard?
I gave to you all I could offer,
though my love you did simply discard.

I know that I can't think about you.

I really must set myself free.
But each time that I thought about you,
did you once ever think about me?

13/09/2001

I Want

I want to be more than your lover,
I want to be more than your friend.
I want to be right there beside you,
I want to play more than pretend.

I want to be seen as your lady,
I want you to crave for my touch.
I want for you to at least love me,
though I fear I am wanting too much.

I want to be your princess,
I want to be your whore,
I want to be so special,
I want you to adore...
each breath that leaves my lips,
the ground on which I walk,
all dreams that I invent,
and all words that I talk.

My wants I'm wanting you to share,
I want!
I want!
is isn't fair!
But tell my wants I wouldn't dare,
when all I wants for you to care.

18/09/2001

Hey Jealousia

I fear to speak my mind,
for I am aware of its treachery.

I fear to say my hurt,
for it is all to ego to bare.

I fear to admit it is mine,
please forgive this translucent gift.
For I know I must love you equal,
though these jealous eyes I just cannot lift.

I'm quite sure I share the surprise,
this confession outcast in your eyes.
Although dear I do realize,
your love I cannot compromise.

I do believe I'm too used to,
shinning on your stage.
My spirit knows,
though ego shows,
it's jealous empty cage.

I can't make head nor tail of,
my cold and envy bed.
As I smash the mirrors glass
where my reflections dare not tread.

10/ 2001

Sweet Good-Byes

"Don't let go",
the broke heart screams.
As salt wet tears fall down in streams.
Drowning out her love's sunbeams...
for now they play for separate teams.

"Don't go now",
the broke heart cries,
"hear me"
wept in compromise,
as all she knows takes off and fly's...
the searing pain of sweet good-byes.

And through this push and pull relay,
the broke heart skips a beat.
Withering light the sparkle fades,
as her special love did know defeat.

Solo confused the silence tore,
all that she could see.
Why was it that,
this thing now lost,
was all but meant to be?

02/01/2002

Relation-Shifts

Friendship for a moment sent, is bound but for a time.
Laughter for a while, may mend a severed twine.
A bit of spit and polish, may help restore the shine.
As a little love and tenderness, may save this starving vine.

To lay and loathe beneath a corpse, which once proclaimed to feel.
Enjoying sour suppers, as if they would be last meal.
To burn under the blazing sun, where flesh begins to peel.
Accepting silent whippings, as you fall face down and squeal.

Affection left to fade into a deep dark cold abyss.
Abstract and void were notions, co-assembled bound to miss.
The web of isolation, slowly pries at once felt bliss.
When a shooting star is falling, for an empty poison kiss.

Derived were scenes of agony, as plots plagued every action.
Terror traits induced so free, for selfish satisfaction.
Shrew so vicious, vile contempt engulfed the lost attraction.
Ascending into status quo, to get a slight reaction.

4/01/2002

US!

Where could you be my love, my all?
For I've sat in this bare cell.
No note has come, no message been,
no sign that all is well.

When last your features smiled on me,
and presence graced my day.
Remarked did you "I'll see you soon",
I wish that were the way.

I'm addicted to me loving you,
this rapture in my heart.
And though detached you too can see,
and feel we're worlds apart.

You've pried me from the place,
I'd once called home inside of you.
How nice it feels to be,
the sticky gum under your shoe.

So quickly to be shuffled off,
your look of slight disgust,
turned pleased to now seem rid of it,
that sticky mess called us.

26/07/02

Yours Is Mine

Staring into silence,
hearing all you failed to see.
Slaying my demons,
you let me slide by.
Accepting my whippings,
you're punished not I.

Fear not!
all fear?
Fear what?
nothing dear!

The shadows you're dreaming,
that stalk me are yours.
You solace then shrouded,
for fear mine endures.

Why can't it be seen?
are all devils lent?
And whom will they follow,
upon your descent.

26/07/2002

Breaking

Lost in a web of deception,

viewed only by blindest of eye.

The fallen now self medicating,

as what did once shimmer now shies...

away from the dreams,
engulfed in the themes,
they tear at the seams,
and we...

are left open to,
all but what we knew,
till there is no us we can see.

No fight can be fought,
for forces too strong,
operate in the darkness around.

And this love they willed die,

will kiss us good bye,

the moment our feet touch the ground.

12/06/2003

Goldstar's Seconds

One speaks ever so softly,
still no one would care to hear.
Drowned out too shy and lonely,
tis' my voice!
wish u were near.
Another day reflected in
one that's come to pass,
A gold star in the waiting,
sits forever second class.

White flag to you I'm waving
in lifeboat adrift I sit.
The sharks now closely circle,
as my final flare is lit.

To standers-by this image,
may be misunderstood,
To the one away and drifting,
Life is far from where it could...

Could or would or should have been.
now far away in lucid dream,
Awaiting all one could have seen,
I wait for you...

Have always been.

30/10/06

Puppet Master

Directions so many,
decisions so few.
My love turmoil tally,
not conquered till true.
Each grain of time slipping,
oh what shall I do?
Unable to exit this game,
which is you.

Pull my pretty puppet limbs,
falling when you drop my strings.
Oh the pleasure that pain brings,
flying on loves broken wings.

Treasures brought,
with truths untold.
Mysterious movement,
with traits that unfold.
Too many false rainbows,
with no pots of gold.
Alone on your stage,
puppeteering got old.

09/03/2003

Flight-Less

I flew for you, then fell so far,
found all's the means to truly scar.
I fell for you and now am lost,
gave all my heart though at what cost?

The whirl we came to know as us,
to be?....
one was so sure!!
So sure..you'd say?
.....??!
Keep my at bay!!!...Throw us away?..
Why?!!..
Why today?!

So come then...crush this butterfly,
she came out just for you!
Drown her deep and hold her down,
her gold heart turn to blue!

Rip off her wings and watch her squirm,
heartbreaking so inept.
And laugh as no one cares to hear,
as onto she is leapt!

Destroyed!
This once acquired taste.
So sad to see,
oh such a waste!
The once loved beauty,
now a paste.

With merely more than concrete floor,

the wings hung high above the door,

now fastened down,

no chance to soar,

trapped in time,

to be no more.

12/07/2004

Closing

If the wind is heard a blowing,
in the sky's once filled with sun,
the stars no longer glowing,
ti's abandoned you've become.
No longer the once useful,
retired on the line,
forgotten for another,
now so tarnished, what did shine.

Will to be subjected,
the willing sacrifice,
such humour found in traps unwrapped
once packaged oh so nice
Betrothed, unto masked fury,
contradiction walks in vein,
such profound dreams now flailing,
in a choice the future slain.

Trusting lamb now tainted,
the wool sublimely pulled,
eyes too blind now recognised,
within where they were fooled.
Alas a sigh, a dry ravine,
a want to flow once more,
determined by an option,
now a proven closing door.

04/11/06

I Never

I stood my place contending,
For a prize, far from my grasp,
blinding eyes of great awareness,
behind a,
smiling lovers mask.

Throughout the time,
spent by thy self,
convinced!,
though I was left on shelf,
alone now coming naturally,
my loving eyes refused to see.

Truth so blatant though declined,
I climbed into my lonely mind,
I blinked so it would disappear,
The smile hiding silent tear.

Hollow, the once filled heart became,
As tears held back, fell down like rain,
Such self denied, time and again,
Confusion ruled, my beauty slain.

1/4/07

Blu Baaalloo

She fell
from the top
of a mountain,
which stretched up to lengths oh so high.
She called
this great peak
Blu Baaalloo,
though still to this day knows not why.

Not known
was how long
she'd been falling,
nor how fast she fell it is true.
Knowing only
she had not yet
touched the ground,
hitting rock bottom from Blu Baaalloo.

With not even a safety line,
the flailing miss no longer blind
remembered she who was divine,
from Blu Baaalloo she'd lost her mind.

Few feet before Blu Baaalloo's core,
she spread her wings & learnt to soar,
her Blu Baaallo she did adore,
& went straight up to fall once more.

29/04/2008

Me "Ow"

In the brightest warmest spaces,
in the depths within my heart,
I keep what makes you special…
so brave,
so warm,
& smart.
For days you would consume me,
and I intern would you.
Lost somewhere you altered,
and I could not see through.
In the multitudes of thoughts,
in the rush within my head.
I piece together what I can,
from all
we saw
and said.
Your silence left me drowning,
your touch evoked my soul,
and wait will I unknowing,
if our two halves you'll make whole.
In the very darkest places,
in the corners of my mind.
I sign my last confession…
Mouth taped,
hands tied,
and blind
Your presence intoxicates me,
floating like a lucid dream.
So blind to the betrayal,
another cat has got the cream.

Bak2sane

You walked in, as if from nowhere,
on that clear warm summers night.
You came into my life,
turning the darkness into light.

You took my hand & breathed me in,
I felt you crawl beneath my skin.
You stole my heart, opened my mind,
it's love like this you're meant to find.

Embarking together we'd journey,
my blind eyes you made see.
We stepped outside the circle,
& dared to make us...we.

Then twisted like a train wreck,
a love that seemed so strong.
Derailed with all its wildest dreams,
when all that could went wrong.

The walls went up, then came to fore,
disguised this opportunist's door.
Crafty yes! Outrageous sure,
so blindly you're pried from the one you adore.

The battle grew so complex,
as the stakes were oh so high.

The only options flight or fight ,
True love versus the lie.

So where can the heart find refuge?
When dreams have fallen through?
When suddenly you kiss good-bye,
to everything you knew.

Shuffled out of shoes,
you'd tried so very hard to fill,
another takes first place now,
as your scores brought back to nil.

Fates fickle finger,
points you down loves lost lonely lane.
Embarking this time solo,
on the journey back to sane!

CHAPTER THREE

Emo Too

You Are

My day,

My night,

My lust,

My fight,

My friend,

My lover,

My soul,

ANOTHER.

With me,

TOGETHER.

In love,

FOREVER.

My thoughts,

My hate,

My love,

My fate.

1998

Measure My Love

Whisked away while dreaming,
dreaming about you.

Contemplating feelings,
old as well as new.

A deep misunderstanding,
a discontented sigh.

A cold and sad remembrance,
of love that wouldn't die.

A million words could not describe,
could not barely compare.

How lonely I am without you,
lonely without you there.

I wish that you could understand,
I wish that you could know.

To have you I'd risk everything,
to any lengths I'd go.

30-08-2000

For A Guy

A smile so enticing,
devious and sly,
a past with so much depth,
one must resist the urge to pry.

A touch possessed by intense strength,
so masculine and firm,
proposing great adventure,
yet removing all concern.

Eyes which pierce right through you,
right through you to the core,
a unique unsolved mystery,
which makes you just want more.

Frustration undeniable,
complete this will not be,
till I'm laying beneath you,
as you come once more for me.

31-01-2001

Empower Me

If I could fly into the heavens,
I'd ask for just one thing...

For you?
For me?
For us.

I'd beg for all my dreams,
to wash over your heart.
For life to give one simple wish.
Our life's mission to start...

The end of separation
A new lease to the nation
Baby pull in at my station!
I'm free.

You'll be there in a mile,
I offer just my smile,
Don't offer me denial,
I'm free.

Empower me with just one kiss,
its choice not chance,
we cannot miss.

Empower us,
with all your strength.
With all your love,
we'll go the length.

03-05-2001

YOU

You are my sun,
which rises up from all dark holes in me.

You are the breath that fills my lungs

You are the cheeky smirk that creeps across my face

You are the silence which fills the coldest air

You are the smooth silk that I wear to sleep

You are the one thing that is so easily missed!

You are a laugh at a funeral,
so necessary yet condemned.

You are a shooting star...
only a myth till seen,

You're a miracle within my dream!

You are a clock without time.

You are a sign without meaning.

YOU ARE EVERYTHING TO ME.

08-06-2001

Waking Truth

As I dream of Wiley woes,
My scattered thoughts,
And silken robes.

I sit
I sly
Though wonder why?
The truth in these I can't expose.

And as I wake my mind it swells,
as familiar sights and smells,
rise to meet my tired eyes,
searching for truth amongst the lies.

And there you lay right next to me.
Sleeping beauty
that I do see.

For there I find,
my truth,
my love.

It's all in you
And it's enough!

13-07-2001

???? What Becomes Of A Kiss????

Kiss me soft and kiss me nice,
Kiss me once then kiss me twice.
Touch my neck brush past my hair,
Kiss my shoulders but don't stop there!
Keep going please don't stop to rest,
As you touch and lick my breast.
Your touch it thrills slide off my gown,
I sense your mouth as you move down.
Your strong hands slide my legs apart,
Your eyes say "Babe it's just the start".
You run your fingers tracing round,
My hot and sticky now wet mound.
You lay me back and disappear,
your warm soft breath I feel draw near.
And then sensations make me squirm,
You pull me in and hold me firm.
You tease and taint as sweet honey,
drips off your lips, please feast on me.
And when I feel I can take no more,
You drive yourself into my core.
Our bodies twist and intertwine,
Our souls connect, what's yours is mine.
And then amongst the sweat and tears,
Two souls become void of all fears.
Then we explode in pure bliss,
what started in....
one simple kiss.

15-07-2001

Late Night Love

Could you please protect me tonight?

Save me from this world of fright.

Take me to a place quiet and safe,

past the realms of time and space.

Take me to where I'll be at peace,

somewhere that I can finally release.

I'm tired of waiting for he who won't come,
I'm ready to find my own place in the sun.

I've loved and was lost in false bottomed
draws,
the cards which I drew, were distractions and
chores.

They say it is better to have loved and then
lost,
but receiving false love always comes with a
cost!

So thank you for giving a love so profound,
my faith in you saved me now I shan't be
bound.

17/07/2001

My Inspiration

To kiss the lips,
that speak the words,
which bring a priceless bond.

To touch a heart,
against all odds,
but not by magic wand.

To seek forgiveness when denied.
To master love accepting pride.
To nowhere need a place to hide.
Is where I find you,
by my side

And where else would I rather be?
In your strong arms?
so warm to me!

And who else would I wait for all...
all my life until I fall?
The simple answer yet again,
is
YOU!
MY BROTHER,
SOUL,
AND FRIEND!

23/08/2001

Miss. U. Ra

I find something is quite amiss,
within my fortress walls,
I seek forever comfort,
though know not from where it calls.
I do believe this thing I crave,
will one day find an end,
But not before I hear from you,
my love and dearest friend.
For only your sweet words,
and lips so soft could make my day,
And although we're so far apart,
my Love I shall not stray!
No matter how far Love you be,
no man nor wench I dare,
Open my soul as I have to thee,
for they could not compare.
So sparkling sun in my eyes,
you are all that I could dream,
and do believe you feel the same,
when your green eyes do gleam.
I love and cherish each and every
hair upon your head,
and hold close to my heart,
the many faces that you shed.
So hurry and be quick in step,
don't leave our love to chill,
as passion like this must be kept,
so not to lose its thrill.

07/10/2001

Hello??

Intrigue and mystery plagued my mind,
upon the time when chance...
slayed this open heart of mine,
in just one simple glance.

Those flaming eyes that burning steel,
shot deeper in one stare,
than great harpoons in history,
As it blazed right through the air.

Though as I peered deep down into,
my freshly opened cage.
The beating sounds within my heart,
were no longer clogged with rage.

It grew with a slight sparkle,
how was I to see the danger?
Another glimpse then introduced,
and then you're not a stranger.

Now at this stage it's hard to tell,
so keep your head and see...
the single in you might turn out,
to much prefer be we!

16/01/2002

Watching Love Lay

With lines that grow deeper,
your brown mane streaks with grey.
Watch do I, sleep do you,
as our time slips away.

How many nights such as this,
have I seen love at rest?
I could have cried an ocean,
for I know love I am blessed.

It shall never be apparent,
to he who doeth sleep.
That every murmur, toss and turn,
my heart does closely keep.

For my words of love are silent,
as my lips cannot define.
The peace which you can bring,
into my separated mind.

Alas I try to turn,
putting all my thoughts to bed.
Hoping that when you awake,
you've felt all my mind has said.

03/05/2003

T*T*S

It never made me love you more,
Nor could it make me less.

Seems unconditional is my way,
With you I must confess.

It never disappointed,
As sweet does taste the same.

For unconditional always is,
It leaves no one or blame,

It never drowned in sorrow,
Each time we'd fall apart
.
I love you unconditional means,

I LOVE YOU ALL-WAYS…

From beginning end to start!

2006

Imagine

Imagine if, time would allow,
a space for you and me,
A place where it would be alright,
somewhere that we could be.

If only you'd imagine,
if only for a while.
How does it make you feel,
does imagining make you smile?

I wish that you'd imagine,
I'd love it to be true.
Returning to a time,
when sweet imaginings all we knew.

Well I know that I imagine,
where the moonlit oceans gleam.
Where my love is all, I could ever wish,
or imagine
or could dream.

30/10/06

Lost & Found

I found what I've been looking for,

Found what I thought I'd lost,

I found myself in eyes so green,

This line I'm glad I crossed,

I could have let you pass me by,

I could have just been friends,

But how could I,
have lived a lie?
for true love never ends.

With you it's not a gamble,

For dreams they can come true,

So thank you so much dearest one,

For letting me love you!

22/3/07

Baaalliiioo

The second our two worlds collide,
light fills space,
all fears subside,
alone no more,
when by your side,
the fit so perfect un denied!

Conjure up a place to be,
Where intent's pure,
& love is free
Keep closed your eyes,
now show to me,
within your kiss, explain...
I'll see!

Breathe in, as if you never knew,
what was before,
now in the blue,
Never mind be it untrue?...
We'll make believe,
Just me and...
You?

21/4/2008

Always & Forever

So lofty are the heights I aim,
for when I am with you…
the outcomes of no consequence,
the journey's all that's true.

Weathering conditions,
be it turbulent or fair.
I'm lost, not for a moment,
knowing you'll always be there.

Discontentment, woe & sorrow,
where you stand it dares not lay.
Love always and forever,
be the destined true hearts way.

Know that time is but the vessel,
for our dreams to stage the dance.
Eternity the backdrop,
for our true love and romance.

In time against the greatest odds,
twin souls can coexist…
so rare this opportunity…
once off
it can't
be missed.

2006-2008

To You

You deserve the ultimate!
In all that life can give!

In health,
In love.
In fall,
In spring.

The very best of everything.

With somber rests
and
sweet sweet dreams,
where flowers grow
near bubbling streams.
And
treasures too,
that's what you're due,
and with this heart,
and love so true
I'll try to give these all to you!!

CHAPTER FOUR

For...

For My Min

There seem to be so many things,
you've sacrificed for me.
Appreciated every time,
these things you gave for free

amongst the many special things,
came love and self respect.
A friend who'll stand the test of time,
my love you won't reject.

To you I can give nothing,
to me you'd give the world.
When I grieve returned to me,
a smile bright and pearled.

You're just so very special,
you won't believe it's true.
There is one thing you must not doubt,
and that's my love for you!

13/01/2001

Dear Sexy

As chubby children we first met,

your unique dress I shan't forget!

But as we grew we always knew,

this friendship's strength was concrete
set.

With vocals of an angel,

a talent wild and rare.

A face so photogenic,

that no model could compare.

By setting an example,

and simply taking charge...

you swung your entire world around,

and without rustling nearby ground,

showed the world what you could do,

and watched them walk by,
as you flew!!

02/ 2001

Mumma

Today I picked a rose for you,
with petals deep and red.

It stood alone,
bleeding in a barren prison of thorn.

It's bloodied scarlet petals,
accentuated by nature's clever fortress.

Thrown was I,
when stabbed and slashed.
By little razor blades.

My cowardliness cried,
"Cease"
"Retreat"

Dare I ignore this unique elegance?

"Ne'r"

I challenged the thorn,
wrestling the prize,

for you.

Victorious.
I ran to your arms.

Then
it was that I realized...

you,

my love are that rose...

You too,
have a beauty unparalleled,
in the cruel cage which you dwell.

You too,
wear a barricade of razor blade thorn.

PROTECTING!

REFLECTING!

Keeping safe the beauty,
which is
you.

And as with the rose,
I am unable to veer,
or ignore.

I feel compelled to find safe passage,
to rescue,
the prize with no comparison,
the solitary elegance.
The individual camouflaged by society.

The rose in the thorn...
you.

Destined To Be
D

Flowing words of wisdom fly,
from your lips to touch the sky.
You teach God's word and know no lie,
offer to us a place to cry.

Before you spoke the world was bare,
my spirit broke needing repair.
Hidden truths with us you share,
embraced are we in Zen Den's lair.

Revealing lies for us to see,
working to find our destiny.
The ego war you fight till free,
protection we have found in thee.

A mind so full of knowledge but always open to,
accept a persons differences no matter what they
do.
A bellow unmistakable, a smile warm and true,
a courage never seen before, discovered within
you.

Please don't lose your faith in me,
I don't think I could bare,
enduring my existence...
without your precious stare!

Thank you for everything
luv-lee
15/06/2001

Hiawotha

If I ever was a mother,

Then a mother I would be…

The type of special mother,

Like you have been to me.

If in darkness I did find,

Those I'd call my own.

I'd shine upon them all the strength,

Like the light on me you've shown.

If I had a chance to be,

Of all things I would choose…

To be the type of mother,

Who's love does not confuse.

If I was blessed to be a mother,

I'd give my all just to become.

Like the one which you have been to me…

Even though you're not my mum.

Thank You

Well first I must say thank you,
for all you stood to bear,
As I was quite impossible,
short fused with wild stare.

And next appreciation,
I do believe your due,
For never giving up on me,
and standing good and true.

I ne'r did think it possible,
for someone for so long,
to carry on intently,
as I tripped out to my song.

And next is my apology,
for being "such a child",
at times when I seem crazy,
I only want to be defiled.

I feel so very lucky,
I'd even dare say blessed,
I don't know how you do it,
I know I'm such a pest!

Yet here you are beside me,
as crazy as it sounds,
You offer the only thing I need,
a love which knows no bounds.

Although at times I seemed mixed up,
I know just what you need,
a lady who is stable,
not a child who will plead!

Well I'm learning to be patient,
as your plate does seem quite full.
You need someone who understands,
who doesn't push and pull.

Please hear me as I say,
there's nothing more that I could want,
than to be a little more reserved,
and act all nonchalant.

But if I change,
I know...
that I'll no longer,
be...
that "crazy girl",
you fell for...
forever yours
Luv Lee.

xoxoxoxoxo

... and not until this day is done
and Salem's final song is sung.

Will we realise why we begun,
and from the dark no longer run.

b*